LET'S L
SINHA

1

VOWELS
and
CONSONANTS

J.B.Disanayaka

Professor Emeritus of Sinhala
BA(Cey) MA(Calif)
PhD(Col) DLit(Col)

First Edition 2003
This Edition 2010

A Sumitha Book

Printed by

SRIDEVI

Sridevi Printers (Pvt) Ltd
27 Pepiliyana Road, Nedimala,
Dehiwala, Sri Lanka.
Tel. 716709

WELCOME TO SINHALA

Learning a second language is an exciting experience. For it takes you to a new world of thought - the world of thought of the people who use it as the first language. As you begin to learn the new language, you begin not only to produce new sounds and write new letters but also to think anew, thus entering a new world of thought.

This is the first book in the series '**Let's Learn Sinhala**'. These books are meant for those who wish to learn Sinhala as a second language: how to speak it and write it. Each book deals with one simple aspect of the patterns that govern the structure of modern Sinhala usage: its sounds, letters, spelling, words, compounds, phrases, clauses and sentences.

Sinhala is one of the two national languages of Sri Lanka. The other language is Tamil, also spoken in the South Indian state of Tamil Nadu. Sinhala is spoken by the Sinhalese who constitute about seventy-five percent of the island's population of seventeen million. Both languages are of Indian origin but belong to two distinct linguistic families: Indo-Aryan and Dravidian.

Sinhala has a writing system that goes back to the third century before Christ. The earliest specimens of Sinhala writing are found in the natural caves inhabited by Buddhist monks in the pre-Christian era. These cave inscriptions were written in the Brahmi script, the script used by the famous Indian emperor Ashoka in engraving his edicts in North India.

Sinhala writing has thus a history that spans over two millennia. The present system of writing is the outcome of processes that were at work over these years. The Sinhala alphabet has now entered the Unicode meant for the computer and includes even a new letter for the sound ‘f’ enabling the Sinhalese to write English words such as ‘fax’, ‘golf’ and ‘giraffe’ with ease.

This book contains 37 units, followed by ‘a Guide to Sinhala words used in the book’. Each Unit introduces just one letter at a time. This letter is always introduced in the context of letters that have been already introduced so that the reader moves gradually from the known to the unknown. It makes learning a new language very easy.

To indicate how Sinhala letters are pronounced, letters of the English alphabet are used. Some letters have been slightly modified to suit Sinhala sounds.

For example, the letter ‘*å*’ stands for the Sinhala sound that is similar to the English sound ‘a’ that occurs at the beginning of English words such as ‘afar’ ‘again’ and ‘away’ and, the letter ‘æ’ stands for the Sinhala sound that is similar to English ‘a’ as in ‘at’ ‘can’ and ‘sat’.

The colon after an English vowel letter indicates that the vowel sound is pronounced long. Thus ‘*a:*’ stands for the English sound ‘ar’ in words such as ‘arch’ ‘arm’ and ‘art’ and, the letter ‘*i:*’ stands for the English sound ‘i’ as in ‘machine’. Other letters that stand for Sinhala sounds are explained in the Units themselves.

The modern Sinhala alphabet as codified in the Unicode contains 61 letters but only 58 are in contemporary use. Of these letters, 37 are introduced in this Book. With these letters you will be able to write almost any Sinhala word that is heard in actual speech. The other letters are necessary to write words taken from Pali and Sanskrit, the two classical languages that had the biggest impact on Sinhala.

Among these letters are 12 vowel letters. These vowel letters are used only at the beginning of a Sinhala word. When such a vowel sound occurs elsewhere in a Sinhala word, a symbol known as a 'vowel stroke' is used. A vowel stroke is called a '*pillå*' in Sinhala. This book, however, does not introduce any vowel strokes. These are introduced in Book 2 of this series.

Letters of the Sinhala alphabet are given names ending in '*yannå*', preceded by the sound that the letter symbolizes. Thus the first letter of the alphabet is called '*a-yannå*' because it is pronounced as 'a' which is similar to the English sound 'u' as in 'up' 'cut. This letter, which is also the first vowel in Sinhala, is one of the most difficult letters to write.

It is the first letter that a Sinhalese child is taught when the alphabet is introduced to the child by one of the parents or by an erudite person, at an auspicious hour, accompanied by religious rites, at a simple ceremony called '*akuru kiyåvi:må'* - reading the letters. Initiation of the child into the alphabet is accompanied by religious rites because letters of the language are considered 'sacred'.

The one who knows letters will become a literate person who can read and write. He can read the religious scriptures and other writings. He will thus become a person who enjoys a special position in a literate society. Ours is an Asian society, which has one of the highest rates of literacy. Writing opens the gateway to the world of knowledge and information.

Welcome to Sinhala!

Learn this language and enjoy a taste of Sinhala!

The Sinhala Alphabet

The Sinhala alphabet in use today has 58 letters: 16 vowels and 42 consonants.

The 16 Vowels

අ	ආ	ඇ	ඈ
ඉ	ඊ	උ	ඌ
ඍ	ඎ	එ	ඒ
ඓ	ඔ	ඕ	ඖ

The 42 Consonants

ක	ඛ	ග	ඝ	ඞ	ඟ
ච	ඡ	ජ	ඣ	ඤ	ඦ
ට	ඨ	ඩ	ඪ	ණ	ඬ
ත	ථ	ද	ධ	න	ඳ
ප	ඵ	බ	භ	ම	ඹ
	ය	ර	ල	ව	
ශ	ෂ	ස	හ	ළ	ෆ
		(අ)ං	(අ)ඃ		

This Book introduces only 37 letters of the Sinhala alphabet:

12 Vowels and 25 Consonants

The 12 Vowels

අ uh	ආ	ඇ	ඈ
ඉ	ඊ	උ	ඌ
එ	ඒ	ඔ	ඕ

The 25 Consonants

ක	ග		ඟ
ච	ජ		
ට ter	ඩ		ඬ
ත	ද	න	ඳ
ප	බ	ම muh	ඹ
ය	ර ruh	ල	ව
ශ	ස suh zuh	හ	ළ
		(අ)ං	

Index to Letters

These 37 letters are introduced in the following order:

1	අ *u*	11	ආ	21	බ	31	ඕ
2	ට *t*	12	ත	22	ඩ	32	ශ
3	ර *r*	13	හ	23	එ	33	ඳ
4	ම *m*	14	ය	24	ක	34	ඬ
5	ස *s*	15	ප	25	ඌ	35	ඹ
6	ඇ	16	ඈ	26	ජ	36	ං
7	ද	17	ල	27	ඒ	37	ෆ
8	ඉ	18	ඊ	28	ච		
9	ග	19	ව	29	ඔ		
10	න	20	උ	30	ෂ		

අ uh 1

This is *a-yannå.*
It is a vowel letter.
It sounds like English ‘u’
as in ‘up’ and ‘under’
‘cup’ and ‘sun’

When Sinhala words are written in English
the letter that will stand for it is

[a]

Thus the Sinhala word for ‘mother’

අම්මා

will be written in English as

[*a m m a*]

This letter comes only at the beginning of a Sinhala word.

It stands for a short vowel.
Its long vowel is : ආ

අ අ අ අ

ට 2

This is *ṭa-yannå*
It is a consonant letter.
It sounds like English ‘t’
as in ‘two’ and ‘tyre’
‘cat’ and ‘rat’

When Sinhala words are written in English
the letter that will stand for it is

[ṭ]

When it comes at the beginning of a Sinhala word
it is pronounced like English ‘tu’ as in ‘tusker’

and will be written as [ṭa]

When it comes elsewhere in a Sinhala word,
it is pronounced like English ‘tter’
as in ‘letter’
and will be written as [ṭå]

[ṭå] ter

අට eight

[*a ṭå*]
uh ter

අට අට අට

අටට at eight, to eight

[*a ṭå ṭå*]

අටට අටට අටට

අට

ර 3

This is *ra-yannå*
It is a consonant letter.
It sounds like English ‘r’
as in ‘red’ and ‘rose’
‘pretty’ and ‘bride’

When Sinhala words are written in English
the letter that will stand for it is

[r]

When it comes at the beginning of a Sinhala word
it is pronounced like English ‘ru’ as in ‘run’

and will be written as [ra]

When it comes elsewhere in a Sinhala word,
it is pronounced like English ‘rror’
as in ‘mirror’

and will be written as [rå]

[rå] rruh

අර that

[*a rå*]
uh rruh

අර

[ra]
ru

රට country, abroad

[*ra ṭå*]
ru tter

රට

ම   4

This is *ma-yannå*
It is a consonant letter.
It sounds like English ‘m’
as in ‘mango’ and ‘monkey’
‘stem’ and ‘arm’

When Sinhala words are written in English
the letter that will stand for it is

[m]

When it comes at the beginning of a Sinhala word
it is pronounced like English ‘mu’ as in ‘mug’

and will be written as [ma]

When it comes elsewhere in a Sinhala word,
it is pronounced like English ‘mmer’
as in ‘summer’

and will be written as [må]

[må]

mmuh

අමර Amara

[*a må rå*]

අමර අමර අමර

අමර අමර

[ma]

muh

මට for me

[*ma ṭå*]

මට මට මට මට

මට

මට

අමර

A må rå

Amara

අමර

අමරට

A må rå ṭå

for Amara

අමරට

මම

ma må

I

මම

මමම

ma må må

I myself

මමම

මටම

ma ṭå må

for me myself

මටම

මම අමර

ma må A må rå

I am Amara

මම අමර

අමර මට

A må rå ma ṭå

Amara is for me

අමර මට

මම රටට

ma må ra ṭå ṭå

I am for the country

මම රටට

අමර අටට

A må rå a ṭå ṭå

Amara at eight

අමර අටට

අමර රට

A må rå rå ṭå

Amara is abroad

අමර රට

ස 5

This is *sa-yannå*
It is a consonant letter.
It sounds like English ‘s’
as in ‘six’ and ‘swan’
‘bus’ and ‘his’

When Sinhala words are written in English
the letter that will stand for it is

[s]

When it comes at the beginning of a Sinhala word
it is pronounced like English ‘su’ as in ‘sun’
and will be written as [sa]

When it comes elsewhere in a Sinhala word,
it is pronounced like English ‘ser’
as in ‘miser’
and will be written as [så]

ස ස ස ස

[så]

zuh.

රස taste, tasty

[*ra så*]

රස රස රස

[sa]

suh

සරම sarong

[*sa rå må*]

සරම සරම සරම

රසට — with taste, tastily

ra så ṭå

රසම — tastiest

ra så må

අර සරම — that sarong

a rå sa rå må

සරම මට — the sarong is for me

sa rå må ma ṭå

අසම සම — without an equal, unique

a så må sa må

සරම අමරට the sarong is for

sa rå må A må rå ṭå Amara

රට සරම foreign sarong

ra ṭå sa rå må

අර අමර that is Amara

a rå A må rå

අර සරම මට that sarong is for me

a rå sa rå må ma ṭå

රට සරම මට the foreign sarong is

ra ṭå sa rå må ma ṭå for me

ඇ 6

This is æ-*yannå.*
It is a vowel letter.
It sounds like English 'a'
as in 'apple' and 'Adam'
'cat' and 'rat'

When Sinhala words are written in English
the letter that will stand for it is

[æ]

It comes only at the beginning of a Sinhala word.
Elsewhere in the word,
it is represented by a vowel stroke:

ැ

It is called æ*då-pillå*

This is a short vowel.

Its long vowel is: ඈ

ඇ ඇ ඇ ඇ

ඇට seeds, bones

æ *ṭå*

ඇර except, having opened

æ *rå*

ඇස eye

æ *så*

ඇම bait

æ *må*

ඇසට for the eye

æ *så* *ṭå*

ද 7

This is *da-yannå*
It is a consonant letter.
It sounds like English ‘th’
as in ‘this’ and ‘ that’
‘feather’ and ‘brother’

When Sinhala words are written in English
the letter that will stand for it is

[d]

When it comes at the beginning of a Sinhala word
it is pronounced like English ‘thu’ as in ‘thus’

and will be written as [da]

When it comes elsewhere in a Sinhala word,
it is pronounced like English ‘ther’
as in ‘leather’
and will be written as [då]

ද ද ද ද

[då]

ඇද crooked

[æ *då*]

ඇද

[da]

දර fire wood

[*da rå*]

දර

ඉ 8

This is *i-yannå.*
It is a vowel letter.
It sounds like English ‘i’
as in ‘insects’ and ‘inside’
‘lip’ and ‘kitten’

When Sinhala words are written in English
the letter that will stand for it is

[i]

It comes only at the beginning of a Sinhala word.
Elsewhere in the word,

it is represented by a vowel stroke.

ි

It is called *is-pillå*

This is a short vowel.

Its long vowel is: ඊ

ඉ ඉ ඉ ඉ

ඉර sun, line

i rå

ඉරට to the sun

i rå ṭå

ඉස head

i så

ඉසට for the head

i så ṭå

ඉම limit, boundary

i må

ග 9

This is *ga-yannå*
It is a consonant letter.
It sounds like English ‘g’
as in ‘goat’ and ‘gate’
‘frog’ and ‘leg’

When Sinhala words are written in English
the letter that will stand for it is

[g]

When it comes at the beginning of a Sinhala word
it is pronounced like English ‘gu’ as in ‘gum’

and will be written as [ga]

When it comes elsewhere in a Sinhala word,
it is pronounced like English ‘ger’
as in ‘finger’
and will be written as [gå]

[gå]

අග end

[*a gå*]

අග අග අග

[ga]

ගස tree

[*ga så*]

ගස ගස ගස

ගම — the village

ga må

ගමට — to the village

ga må ṭå

මග — road, path, way

ma gå

අගට — at the end, to the end

a gå ṭå

අගටම — at the very end, to the very end

a gå ṭå må

ගම රට — home town

ga må ra ṭå

අර ගස — that tree

a rå ga så

අර ගසට — for that tree, to that tree

a rå ga så ṭå

ගස දරට — the tree is for firewood

ga så da rå ṭå

ඇද ගස — the crooked tree

æ *då ga så*

න 10

It is *na-yannå*
It is a consonant letter.
It sounds like English ‘n’
as in ‘nose’ and ‘net’
‘pen’ and ‘fan’

When Sinhala words are written in English
the letter that will stand for it is

[n]

When it come at the beginning of a Sinhala word
it is pronounced like English ‘nu’ as in ‘nut’

and will be written as [na]

When it comes elsewhere in a Sinhala word,
it is pronounced like English ‘nner’
as in ‘banner’
and will be written as [nå]

න න න න

[nå]

ගන thick

[*ga nå*]

ගන ගන ගන

[na]

නම name

[*na må*]

නම නම නම

නම ගම — name and address

na må ga må

නගර — cities, towns

na gå rå

අග නගර — chief cities, capitals

a gå na gå rå

නටන — vb. dancing

na ṭå nå

මසන — vb. sewing

ma så nå

නටන අමර Amara who is dancing

na ṭå nå A må rå

නටන ගස the tree that is dancing

na ṭå nå ga så

අමර ඉරන ගස the tree Amara

a må rå i rå nå ga så is sawing

අමර මසන සරම the sarong

a må rå ma så nå sa rå må Amara is sewing

සරම මසන අමර Amara who is

sa rå må ma så nå A må rå sewing the sarong

ආ 11

This is *a:-yannå.*
It is a vowel letter.
It sounds like English ‘ar’
as in ‘arm’ and ‘art’
‘car’ and ‘park’

When Sinhala words are written in English
the letter that will stand for it is

[a:]

It comes only at the beginning of a Sinhala word.
Elsewhere in the word,
it is represented by a vowel stroke:

ා

It is called æ*lå-pillå*

ආ ආ ආ ආ

ආගම religion

a: gå må

ආසන seats

a: så nå

ආදර love, affection

a: då rå

ආර stream, brook, style

a: rå

ආන holder for mats

a: nå

ත 12

It is *ta-yannå*
It is a consonant letter.
It sounds like English ‘th’
as in ‘thorn’ and ‘three’
‘teeth’ and ‘cloth’

When Sinhala words are written in English
the letter that will stand for it is

[t]

When it comes at the beginning of a Sinhala word
it is pronounced like English ‘thu’ as in ‘thumb’

and will be written as [ta]

When it comes elsewhere in a Sinhala word,
it is pronounced like English ‘ther’
as in ‘Esther’
and will be written as [tå]

ත ත ත ත

[tå]

අත hand, arm, direction

[*a tå*]

අත අත අත

[ta]

තද tight, bold, firm

[*ta då*]

තද තද තද

තර fat

ta rå

තම one's own

ta må

තරම size

ta rå må

දත tooth

da tå

සත cents

sa tå

තම අත   one's own hand

ta må a tå

තම රට   one's own country

ta må ra ṭå

තම සරම   one's own sarong

ta må sa rå må

සතර අත   the four directions

sa tå rå a tå

අතර මග   half way

a tå rå ma gå

හ 13

This is *ha-yannå*
It is a consonant letter.
It sounds like English 'h'
as in 'hen' and 'hat'

When Sinhala words are written in English
the letter that will stand for it is

[h]

When it comes at the beginning of a Sinhala word
it is pronounced like English 'hu' as in 'hut'

and will be written as [ha]

When it comes elsewhere in a Sinhala word,
it is pronounced like English 'her'
as in 'herb'
and will be written as [hå]

හ හ හ හ

[hå]

ඉහ head

[*i* *hå*]

ඉහ ඉහ ඉහ

[ha]

හත seven

[*ha* *tå*]

හත හත හත

හතර four

ha tå rå

රහස secret

ra ha så

මහත fat

ma ha tå

සමහර some

sa må ha rå

හරහට across

ha rå ha ṭå

දහ හතර fourteen

da ha ha tå rå

දහ හත seventeen

da ha ha tå

දහ අට eighteen

da ha a ṭå

දහ දහස ten thousand

da ha da ha så

දහ අට දහස eighteen thousand

da ha a ṭå da ha så

ය 14

This is *ya-yannå*
It is a consonant letter.
It sounds like English 'y'
as in 'yellow' and 'yolk'
'toy' and 'boy'

When Sinhala words are written in English
the letter that will stand for it is

[y]

When it comes at the beginning of a Sinhala word
it is pronounced like English 'you' as in 'young'
and will be written as [ya]

When it comes elsewhere in a Sinhala word,
it is pronounced like English 'ear'
as in 'near'
and will be written as [yå]

ය ය ය ය

[yå]

හය six

[*ha yå*]

හය හය හය

[ya]

යට below, under

[*ya ṭå*]

යට යට යට

යස fine, wonderful

ya så

යසට well, wonderfully

ya så ṭå

යන vb. going

ya nå

අය people, income

a yå

වයස age

va yå så

සමහර අය some people

sa må ha rå a yå

මහත අය fat people

ma ha tå a yå

රට යන අය people going abroad

ra ṭå ya nå a yå

වයසට යන අය

va yå så ṭå ya nå a yå

people growing old

රට යන සමහර අය

ra ṭå ya nå sa må ha rå a yå

some people who go abroad

ප 15

This is *pa-yannå*
It is a consonant letter.
It sounds like English ‘p’
as in ‘parrot’ and ‘peacock’
‘lip’ and ‘cup’

When Sinhala words are written in English
the letter that will stand for it is’

[p]

When it comes at the beginning of a Sinhala word
it is pronounced like English ‘pu’ as in ‘puppy’
and will be written as [pa]

When it comes elsewhere in a Sinhala word,
it is pronounced like English ‘pper’
as in ‘grass hopper’
and will be written as [på]

ප ප ප ප

[på]

අපට for us

[*a på ṭå*]

අපට අපට අපට

[pa]

පහ five

[*pa ha*]

පහ පහ පහ

පය foot

pa yå

පට silk

pa ṭå

පනහ fifty

pa nå ha

පහත low, below

pa ha tå

පහන lamp

pa ha nå

අත පය	hand and foot, limbs
a tå pa yå	
සත පනහ	fifty cents
sa tå pa nå ha	
සත පනහට	for fifty cents
sa tå pa nå ha ṭå	
පහත රට	low country
pa ha tå ra ṭå	
පහන යට	under the lamp
pa ha nå ya ṭå	

ඈ 16

This is æ*:yannå.*
It is a vowel letter.
It sounds like English ‘a’
as in ‘ant’ and ‘ass’
‘hand’ and ‘van’ ·

When Sinhala words are written in English
the letter that will stand for it is

[æ:]

It comes only at the beginning of a Sinhala word.
Elsewhere in the word,
it is represented by a vowel stroke:

ෑ

It is called *dik æda-pillå*

ඈ ඈ ඈ ඈ

ඇය

she

æ:

ඇයට

for her, to her

æ: *ṭå*

ඈත

far away, distant

æ: *tå*

ඈතට

at a distance,

to a distance

æ: *tå ṭå*

ඈතම

most distant

æ: *tå må*

ල 17

This is *la-yannå*
It is a consonant letter.
It sounds like English ‘l’
as in ‘lion’ and ‘leg’
‘eel’ and ‘doll’

When Sinhala words are written in English
the letter that will stand for it is

[l]

When it comes at the beginning of a Sinhala word
it is pronounced like English ‘lu’ as in ‘luck’
and will be written as [la]

When it comes elsewhere in a Sinhala word,
it is pronounced like English ‘lor’
as in ‘tailor’
and will be written as [lå]

ල ල ල ල

[lå]

මල flower

[*ma lå*]

මල මල මල

[la]

ලප scars, marks

[*la på*]

ලප ලප ලප

අල — yams, potatoes

a lå

ගල — rock, stone

ga lå

තල — sesame, gingelly, talipot blade

ta lå

අසල — near by, close by

a så lå

සරල — simple

sa rå lå

රට අල a kind of yam

ra ṭå a lå

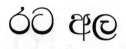

ගල යට under the rock

ga lå ya ṭå

තල මල talipot flower

ta lå ma lå

ගල අසල near the rock

ga lå a så lå

ලට පට tit bits, rubbish, nonsense

la ṭå pa ṭå

ඊ 18

This is *i : yannå.*
It is a vowel letter.
It sounds like English ‘ee’
as in ‘eel’ and ‘bee’
‘tree’ and ‘seem’

When Sinhala words are written in English
the letter that will stand for it is

[i:]

It comes only at the beginning of a Sinhala word.
Elsewhere in the word,
it is represented by a vowel stroke

ී

It is called *dik is-pillå*

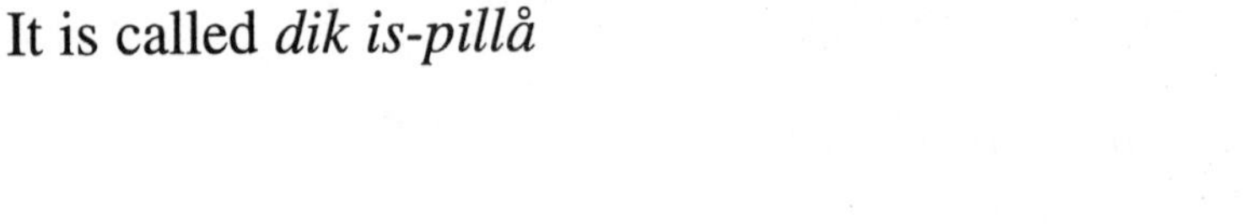

ඊය arrow

i: yå

ඊට for it, for that

i: ṭå

ඊ තල arrows

i: ta lå

ඊ තලය arrow

i: ta lå yå

ඊ ගස arrow

i: ga så

ව 19

This is *va-yannå*
It is a consonant letter.
It sounds like English ‘v’ or ‘w’
as in ‘violin’ and ‘vase’
‘wall’ and ‘window’

When Sinhala words are written in English
the letter that will stand for it is

[v]

When it comes at the beginning of a Sinhala word
it is pronounced like English ‘wo’ as in ‘wonder’
and will be written as [va]

When it comes elsewhere in a Sinhala word,
it is pronounced like English ‘ver’
as in ‘river’
and will be written as [vå]

[vå]

නව new, nine

[*na vå*]

නව නව නව

[va]

වම left

[*va må*]

වම වම වම

වට

va ṭå

round

වනය

va nå yå

jungle, forest

විස

va så

poison

දවස

da vå så

day

හවස

ha vå så

evening

වදු මල   shoe flower

va då ma lå

වන මල   wild flower

va nå ma lå

අදු දවස   this day, today

a då da vå så

අදු හවස   this evening

a då ha vå så

අදු හවස හතරට

a då ha vå så ha tå rå ṭå

at four this evening

උ 20

This is *u-yannå.*
It is a vowel letter.
It sounds like English ‘u’
as in ‘put’ and ‘cushion’
‘push’ and ‘pull’

When Sinhala words are written in English
the letter that will stand for it is

[u]

It comes only at the beginning of a Sinhala word. Elsewhere in the word, it is represented by one of the vowel stroke:

ු ු

It is called *pa:-pilla*

This is a short vowel.

Its long vowel is ඌ

උ උ උ උ

උස — tall, height

u sȧ

උල — point

u lȧ

උයන — park, garden

u yȧ nȧ — vb. cooking

උදය — morning

u dȧ yȧ

උරය — bag, case

u rȧ yȧ

බ 21

This is *ba-yannå*
It is a consonant letter.
It sounds like English ‘b’
as in ‘boy’ and ‘ball’
‘nib’ and ‘cab’

When Sinhala words are written in English
the letter that will stand for it is

[b]

When it comes at the beginning of a Sinhala word
it is pronounced like English ‘bu’ as in ‘bus’
and will be written as [ba]

When it comes elsewhere in a Sinhala word,
it is pronounced like English ‘bour’
as in ‘harbour’
and will be written as [bå]

[bå]

අඹ mustard

[*a bå*]

අඹ අඹ අඹ

[ba]

බට reeds, pipes

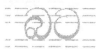

[*ba ṭå*]

බට බට බට

බය fear, scare

ba yå

බර weight, heavy

ba rå

බතල sweet potatoes

ba tå lå

බල power, kind of fish

ba lå

බස language

ba så

අබ මල — mustard flower

a bå ma lå

බල තල — powers

ba lå ta lå

තම බස — one's language

ta må ba så

තද බල — severe, critical

ta då ba lå

හර බර — profound, heavy

ha rå ba rå

ඩ 22

This is *ḍa-yannå*
It is a consonant letter.
It sounds like English 'd'
as in 'dog' and 'doll'
'head' and 'bed'

When Sinhala words are written in English
the letter that will stand for it is

[ḍ]

When it comes at the beginning of a Sinhala word
it is pronounced like English 'du' as in 'duck'
and will be written as [ḍa]

When it comes elsewhere in a Sinhala word,
it is pronounced like English 'dder'
as in 'ladder'
and it will be written as [ḍå]

ඩ ඩ ඩ ඩ

[då]

උඩ රට up country

[*u ḍå ra ṭå*]

උඩ රට උඩ රට

[da]

ඩයනා Diana

[*ḍa ya na*]

ඩයනා ඩයනා

එ 23

This is *e-yannå.*
It is a vowel letter.
It sounds like English 'e'
as in 'egg' and 'elephant'
'nest' and 'teddy'

When Sinhala words are written in English
the letter that will stand for it is

[e]

It comes only at the beginning of a Sinhala word.
Elsewhere in the word,
it is represented by a vowel stroke:

ෙ

It is called *kombuvå*

This is a short vowel.

Its long vowel is: ඒ

එ එ එ එ

එන — vb. coming, next

e nå

එම — that

e må

එය — that thing, that one

e yå

එන අය — those who are coming

e nå a yå

එතන — there, in that place

e tå nå

ක 24

This is *ka-yannå*
It is a consonant letter.
It sounds like English 'k' or 'c'
as in 'kite' and 'book'
'cat and 'camel'

When Sinhala words are written in English
the letter that will stand for it is

[k]

When it comes at the beginning of a Sinhala word
it is pronounced like English 'co' as in 'cow'

and it will be written as [ka]

When it comes elsewhere in a Sinhala word,
it is pronounced like English 'cker'
as in 'wood pecker'

and it will be written as [kå]

ක ක ක ක

[kå]

එක one

[*e kå*]

එක එක එක

[ka]

කට mouth

[*ka ṭå*]

කට කට කට

කන — ear, vb.eating

ka nå

කර — neck

ka rå

කහ — turmeric, saffron yellow

ka ha

කඩල — gram

ka ḍå lå

නරක — bad

na rå kå

කරදර troubles

ka rå då rå

කරවල dry fish

ka rå vå lå

කලබල disturbances

ka lå bå lå

ඝනකම thick, thickness

ga nå kå må

කහ මදය yolk of an egg

ka ha ma då yå

ඌ 25

This is *u:-yannå.*
It is a vowel letter.
It sounds like English ‘oo’
as in ‘ooze’ and ‘school’
‘pool’ and ‘stool’

When Sinhala words are written in English the letter that will stand for it is

[u:]

It comes only at the beginning of a Sinhala word. Elsewhere in the word, it is represented by one of the following vowel strokes:

ූ ෟ

It is called *dik pa: pillå*

ඌ ඌ ඌ ඌ

ඌ — he, it (for animals)

u:

ඌම — he himself (for animals)

u: må

ඌට — for him (for animals)

u: ṭå

ඌව — Uva, name of one of the nine provinces of Sri Lanka

u: vå

ඌන — deficient, minus

u: nå

ඒ 26

This is *e: yannå.*
It is a vowel letter.
It sounds somewhat like English ‘a’
as in ‘ate’ and ‘ache’
‘gate and ‘rate’

When Sinhala words are written in English
the letter that will stand for it is

[e:]

It comes only at the beginning of a Sinhala word.
Elsewhere in the word, it is represented by a vowel stroke which contains two parts;
the *kombuvå* followed by a flag or cap

ෙ ්

ඒ that

e:

ඒක that thing, that one

e: kå

ඒ නම that name

e: na må

ඒ මල that flower

e: ma lå

ඒකට for that

e: kå ṭå

ජ 27

This is *ja-yannå*
It is a consonant letter.
It sounds like English ‘j’ or ‘dge’
as in ‘jam’ and ‘jackal’
‘bridge’ and ‘badge’

When Sinhala words are written in English
the letter that will stand for it is

[j]

When it comes at the beginning of a Sinhala word
it is pronounced like English ‘ju’ as in ‘jump’
and will be written as [ja]

When it comes elsewhere in a Sinhala word,
it is pronounced like English ‘dger’
as in ‘badger’
and it will be written as [jå]

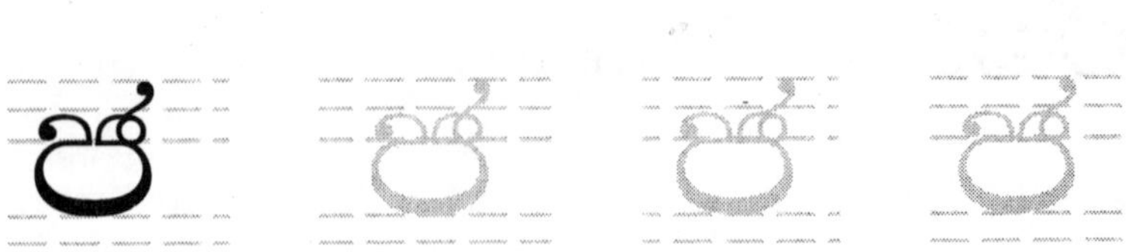

[jå]

රජ king

[*ra jå*]

රජ රජ රජ

[ja]

ජය victory

[*ja yå*]

ජය ජය ජය

ච 28

This is *cha-yannå*
It is a consonant letter.
It sounds like English ‘ch’
as in ‘chicken’ and ‘church’
‘ostrich’ and ‘coach’

When Sinhala words are written in English
the letters that will stand for it are
[ch]

When it comes at the beginning of a Sinhala word
it is pronounced like English ‘chu’ as in ‘chum’
and it will be written as [cha]

When it comes elsewhere in a Sinhala word,
it is pronounced like English ‘cher’
as in ‘archer’
and it will be written as [chå]

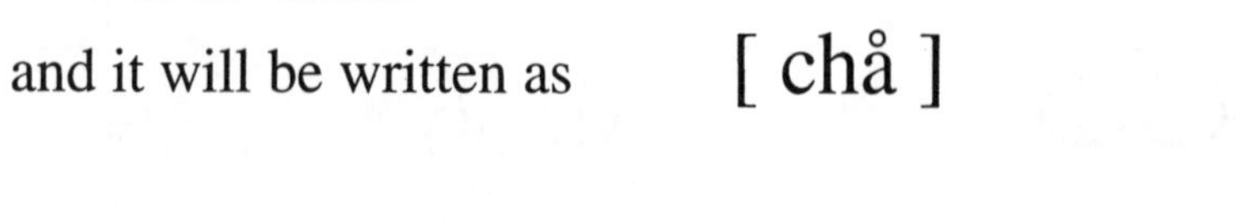

[chå]

පච big lies

[*pa chå*]

පච පච පච

[cha]

චට පට noise of crackers

[*cha ṭå* *pa ṭå*]

චට පට චට පට

ඔ 29

This is *o-yannå.*
It is a vowel letter.
It sounds like English ‘o’
as in ‘pond’ and ‘poppy’

When Sinhala words are written in English
the letter that will stand for it is

[o]

It comes only at the beginning of a Sinhala word. Elsewhere in the word, it is represented by a vowel stroke which contains two parts

ෙ ා

the *kombuvå* followed by the æ*lå-pillå*

This is a short vowel.

Its long vowel is: ඕ

ඔ ඔ ඔ ඔ

ඔය this, (near you), stream

o yå

ඔතන this place (near you)

o tå nå

ඔය නම this name

o yå na må

මහ ඔය Maha Oya, name of a river

ma ha o yå in Sri Lanka

ඔබ you (formal)

o bå

ෂ 30

This is *sha-yannå.*
It is a consonant letter.
It sounds like English 'sh'
as in 'shirt' and 'shoe'
'fish' and 'dish'

When Sinhala words are written in English
the letters that will stand for it are

[sh]

When it comes at the beginning of a Sinhala word
it is pronounced like English 'shu' as in 'shuttle'
and will be written as [sha]

When it comes elsewhere in a Sinhala word,
it is pronounced like English 'sher'
as in 'usher'
and it will be written as [shå]

ෂ ෂ ෂ ෂ

[shå]

දශම

decimal

[*da shå må*]

දශම දශම දශම

[sha]

ශතකය

century

[*sha tå kå yå*]

ශතකය ශතකය

ඕ 31

This is *o:-yannå.*
It is a vowel letter.
It sounds somewhat like English ‘o’
as in ‘nose’ and ‘rose’

When Sinhala words are written in English
the letter that will stand for it is

[o:]

It comes only at the beginning of a Sinhala word. Elsewhere in the word, it is represented by a vowel stroke which contains two parts:

the *kombuvå* followed by the æ*lå-pillå* with a flag.

ෙ ා්

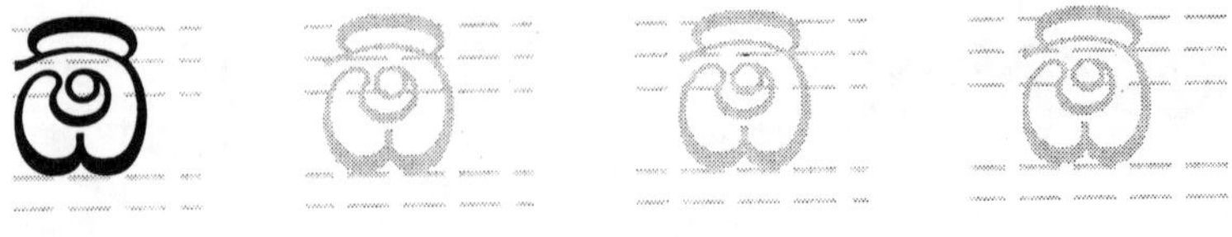

ඕක this thing, (near you)

o: kå

ඕකට for that thing (near you), for that

o: kå ṭå

ඕඩරය the order (customer's request)

o: ḍå rå yå

ඕවරය over (in cricket)

o: vå rå yå

ඟ 32

This looks like *ga-yannå* ,but with a difference.
It stands for a sound not found in English.
It is a strange sound found only
in a few languages like Sinhala.

If you can pronounce
the two sounds [n] and [g]
not after one another as in the English word
'finger' [fin-ger]
but at the same time
you may produce the sound for which it stands.

It never comes at the beginning of a word.

When Sinhala words are written in English
the letters that will stand for it are

[ň g]

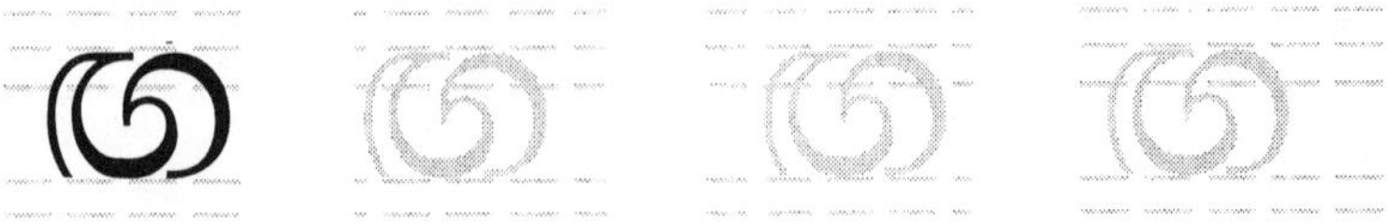

අඟ horn

a ňgå

ඇඟ body

æ *ňgå*

ඉඟ waist

i ňgå

ගඟ river

ga ňgå

දඟරය coil

da ňgå rå yå

ඳ 33

It looks like *da-yannå,* but with a difference.
It stands for a sound not found in English.
It is a strange sound found only
in a few languages like Sinhala.

If you can pronounce
the two sounds [n] and [the]
not after one another as in the English words
'can they' [ca-n the-y]
but at the same time
you may produce the sound for which it stands.

It never comes at the beginning of a word.

When Sinhala words are written in English
the letters that will stand for it are

[ň d]

ඇඳ bed

æ *ňdå*

කඳ body, trunk

ka ňdå

ගඳ bad smell

ga ňdå

හඳ moon

ha ňdå

හඳහන horoscope

ha ňdå ha nå

ඬ 34

It looks like *ḍa-yannå,* but with a difference.
It stands for a sound not found in English.
It is a strange sound found only
in a few languages like Sinhala.

If you can pronounce
the two sounds [n] and [d]
not after one another as in the English word
'London' [Lon-don]
but at the same time
you may produce the sound for which it stands.

It never comes at the beginning of a word.

When Sinhala words are written in English
the letters that will stand for it are

[n̆ ḍ]

ඬ ඬ ඬ ඬ

අඬ noise, sound

a ňḍå

හඬ noise, sound

ha ňḍå

අඬන vb. crying

a ňḍå nå

අඬන අය those who cry

a ňḍå nå a yå

අඬලන vb. crying (of birds)

a ňḍå la nå

ඹ 35

This is like both *ma-yannå* and *ba-yannå*
put together into one.
It stands for a sound not found in English.
It is a strange sound found only
in a few languages like Sinhala.

If you can pronounce
the two sounds [m] and [b]
not after one another as in the English word
'number' [num-ber]
but at the same time
you may produce the sound for which it stands.

It never comes at the beginning of a word.

When Sinhala words are written in English
the letters that will stand for it are

[m̆b]

ඹ ඹ ඹ ඹ

අඹ mango

a m̆bå

කඹය rope

ka m̆bå yå

තඹ copper

ta m̆bå

සරඹ physical exercices

sa rå m̆bå

දඹල kind of beans,

da m̆bå lå winged-beans

ං 36

This is *binduvå.*
It is a consonant letter.
It sounds like English ‘ng’
as in ‘king’ and ‘sing’

It is a consonant with a difference.

It never comes at the beginning of a word.

It can never be followed by a vowel.

When Sinhala words are written in English

the letters that will stand for it are

[ng]

ං ං ං ං

අං horns

a ng

අංකය number

a ng kå yå

මං I

ma ng

මංගල auspicious

ma ng gå lå

සංගමය society

sa ng gå må yå

ෆ 37

This is *fa-yannå.*
It is a newcomer.
It came to stand for English ‘f’
as in ‘fish’ and ‘fox’
‘sniff’ and ‘leaf’

When Sinhala words are written in English
the very same English letter is used:
[f]

When it comes at the beginning of a Sinhala word
it is pronounced like English ‘fu’ as in ‘fun’

and it will be written as [fa]

When it comes elsewhere in a Sinhala word,
it is pronounced like English ‘fer’
as in ‘buffer’
and it will be written as:[få]

ෆ ෆ ෆ ෆ

GUIDE TO SINHALA WORDS USED IN THIS BOOK

අ

අං	horns
අංකය	number
අග	end
අගට	at the end, to the end
අගටම	at the very end, to the very end
අග නගර	chief cities, capitals
අඟ	horn
අට	eight
අටට	at eight, to eight
අඬ	noise, sound
අඬන	vb. crying
අඬලන	vb. crying (of birds)
අත	hand, arm, direction
අත පය	hand and foot, limbs
අතර මග	half way
අපට	for us
අබ	mustard
අමර	Amara, name of a male
අඹ	mango
අය	people, income
අර	that
අල	potatoes, yams
අසම සම	without an equal, unique
අසල	near by, close by

ආ

ආගම	religion
ආදර	love, affection
ආර	brook, stream, style
ආසන	seats

ඇ

ඇඟ	body
ඇට	seeds, bones
ඇද	crooked

ඇඳ	bed
ඇම	baits
ඇර	except, having opened
ඇස	eye
ඇසට	for the eye

ඈ

ඈ	she
ඈට	for her
ඈත	far away, distant
ඈතට	at a distance, to a distance
ඈතම	most distant

ඉ

ඉඟ	waist
ඉම	limit, boundary
ඉර	sun, line
ඉරන	vb. sawing
ඉස	head
ඉසට	for the head
ඉහ	head

ඊ

ඊට	for it
ඊ ගස	arrow
ඊ තල	arrows
ඊ තලය	arrow
ඊය	arrow

උ

උඩ	up, above
උඩ රට	up country
උදය	morning
උයන	park, garden, vb. cooking
උරය	bag, case
උල	point
උස	tall, height

ඌ

ඌ	he (for animals)
ඌට	for him (for animals)
ඌන	deficient, minus
ඌම	he himself (for animals)
ඌව	Uva, name of province in Sri Lanka

එ

එක	one
එතන	in that place, there
එන	vb. coming, next
එය	that thing, it

ඒ

ඒ	that
ඒක	that thing, it
ඒකට	for that thing, for it

ඔ

ඔතන	this place (near you)
ඔබ	you (formal)
ඔය	this (near you), stream

ඕ

ඕක	this thing (near you)
ඕකට	for this thing (near you)
ඕඩරය	order (customer's request)
ඕවරය	over (in cricket)

ක

කට	mouth
කඩල	gram
කන	ear, vb. eating
කඳ	body, trunk
කඹය	rope
කර	neck
කරදර	troubles
කරවල	dry fish

කහ	turmeric, saffron, yellow
කහ මදය	yolk of an egg
කලබල	disturbances

ග

ගඟ	river
ගන	thick
ගනකම	thickness
ගඳ	bad smell
ගම	víllage
ගමට	to the village
ගම රට	home town
ගල	rock, stone
ගස	tree

ච

චට පට	noise of crackers

ජ

ජය	victory

ත

තද	thick, bold, firm
තද බල	severe, critical
තම	own's own
තඹ	copper
තර	fat
තරම	size
තල	sesame, gingelly, talipot, blade

ද

දඟරය	coil
දත	tooth
දඹල	winged-beans
දර	fire wood
දවස	day
දශම	decimal
දහ	ten

දහ අට	eighteen
දහ අට දහස	eighteen thousand
දහ දහස	ten thousand
දහස	thousand
දහ හත	seventeen
දහ හතර	fourteen

න

නටන	vb. dancing
නගර	cities, towns
නම	name
නම ගම	name and address
නරක	bad
නව	new, nine

ප

පච	lies
පට	silk
පනහ	fifty
පය	foot
පහ	five
පහත	low, below
පහත රට	low country
පහන	lamp

බ

බට	reeds, pipes
බතල	sweet potatoes
බය	fear, scare
බර	heavy, weight
බල	powers, kind of fish
බල තල	powers
බස	language

ම

මං	I
මංගල	auspicious
මග	road, path, way

මට	for me, to me
මටම	for me myself
මම	I
මමම	I myself
මල	flower
මසන	vb. sewing
මහ	big, huge
මහ ඔය	name of a river
මහත	fat

ය

යට	under, below
යන	vb. going
යස	fine, wonderful
යසට	well, wonderfully

ර

රට	country, foreign
රජ	king
රස	taste, tasty
රසට	with taste, tastily
රසම	tastiest
රහස	secret

ල

ලට පට	tit bits, rubbish, nonsense
ලප	marks, scars

ව

වට	round
වද මල	shoe-flower
වනය	forest, jungle
වම	left
වයස	age
වස	poison

ශ

ශතකය	century

ස

සංගමය	society
සත	cents
සත පනහ	fifty cents
සතර	four
සමහර	some
සරම	sarong
සරඹ	physical exercises
සරල	simple

හ

හත	seven
හතර	four
හඳ	moon
හඳහන	horoscope
හය	six
හර බර	profound, deep
හරහට	across
හවස	evening

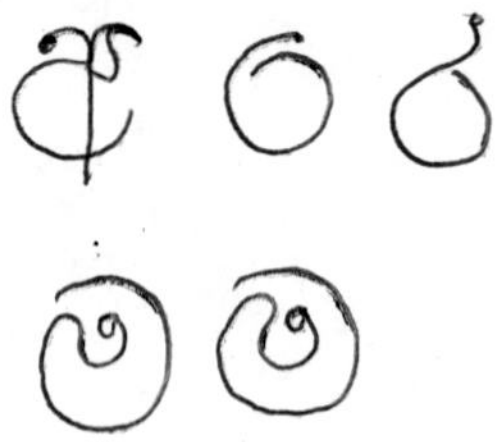